DAYBREAK

DAYBREAK
JACK HAYFORD

Tyndale House Publishers, Inc.
Wheaton, Illinois

To Anna, my dear lady and understanding wife, whose
practical wisdom has blessed me and our four children. I first
came to love her because she was always so genuinely real
and loving. And she has stayed that way because she walks
with Jesus every day.

All Bible quotations are taken from *The Living
Bible,* copyright 1971 by Tyndale House Publishers,
Wheaton, Illinois, unless indicated as being from
The Holy Bible, New King James Version (NKJV),
copyright 1979, 1980, 1982 by Thomas Nelson,
Inc., Nashville, Tennessee.

Third printing, Tyndale House edition, July 1988

Library of Congress Catalog Card Number 86-51350
ISBN 0-8423-0524-6
Copyright 1984 by Jack Hayford
All rights reserved
Printed in the United States of America

CONTENTS

INTRODUCTION

There is something of new hope in a
sunrise.

God made sunrises so that they would be that
way. He wanted us to see each new day as a new
opportunity—a brand new span of time, alive
with promise and possibilities.

Daybreak.

Broken open like *a gift*, surprising our hearts
with God's provision. Broken open like *an egg*,
with life bursting forth as simply and brightly as
a yellow chick. Broken open like *the sky*, with
shafts of light splitting dewdrops into rainbows
of promise.

Promises!

May your strength match the length of your days! (Deuteronomy 33:25)

This is the day the Lord has made. (Psalm 118:24)

His lovingkindness begins afresh each day. (Lamentations 3:23)

Daybreak can become a time of your life's greatest rendezvous—the regular meeting time between you and your Creator. Eden is recovered as the Redeemer and his beloved redeemed child fellowship again.

Daybreak is potentially your life's greatest planning time—the entry of a finite soul into the infinite God's chartroom. In his presence we can receive wisdom for planning each day to fit perfectly into his master plan.

DAYBREAK
Sunshine or cloud, raindrop or dew,
      Lightning with thunder, or meadow-
      like calm;
Foggy and gray or crystalline view,
      Glare on the tundra or glint on the
      palm.
Whatever weather, wherever I be,
      Shadows depart as the night drifts
      away.
Earth's spinning orb turns me to thee,
      Son of God risen, I rise to thy day.
Fearful my heart or fevered my brow,

Introduction

> Troubled my spirit at this day's
> sunrise;
> Naught of this world ties my soul now.
> When daybreak's with Jesus,
> I mount to the skies!

Let us learn together to break open the gift of each day, walking with Jesus into it and through it, to his marvelous tomorrows.

CHAPTER ONE
A MORNING WAKE-UP CALL

I sat on the edge of the bed, rubbing my eyes. The bedside alarm had just announced the time—6:00 A.M.—the time I got up every day to pray. And yet I was about to receive a startling word from God about my neglect of a specific aspect of prayer.

Without any forewarning, and without any expectation on my part that he would speak to me, the Lord breathed these words from his heart into my mind: "You have forgotten the discipline of a daily devotional habit."

I sat there, thoughtfully weighing the significance of the words. Although they lacked condemnation, they carried a sense of urgency. I could feel a weight on my heart as understanding and revelation spread over me. *I have, indeed,* I thought. *These words are true.*

I was surprised and somewhat stunned, but in such a refreshingly blessed way that it delights me to tell about it all over again. You see, it wasn't as though I didn't already have a prayer habit. God had directly addressed me about my devotional habit—and I instantly understood his intent. The difference was crucial as it related to my—and to anyone's—walk with Christ. Let me tell you about it.

EARLY LESSONS

I came to know Jesus as my Savior while I was a boy, and in my teenage years I experienced the blessing of learning early the wisdom and practice of daily devotions, which usually involved a time set aside for regular Bible reading and prayer. This habit extended into my adult years, which is why that early morning visit from God was so remarkable . . . he spoke to me at a time when I was, in fact, getting up to do just that—pray. But God was gently correcting me with explicit counsel that while I had not forgotten about prayer completely, I had forgotten about an aspect of prayer.

And that was a significant distinction!

For several years prior to that special morning, prayer had been a growing, mushrooming reality in my personal life and my ministry. So it was understandable, and somewhat comforting, that the Lord hadn't said, "You've forgotten to pray." He had heard my many prayers and had often

taught me lessons in and about praying. In fact,
the preceding decade had involved the most
expansive and expanding period of my life in
terms of faith-filled prayer, spirit-filled worship
and praise, and divinely energized intercession
and spiritual warfare. All of those facets of
prayer had become very special to me, and as I
grew in understanding them I taught them to
others.

By the time the Lord spoke to me that morning
about forgetting the devotional habit, I had au-
thored a widely distributed book on prayer, led
my congregation up pathways of prayerful
pursuit, hosted a three-year television series of
teachings on prayer, and committed myself to
being a person of faith and bold praying.

And yet . . .

In the midst of it all, the Lord himself was
calling me to something I had unintentionally
begun to overlook. He was not discounting what
I had learned, but he was insisting that I not
forget to exercise the original basic in prayer:
being with him.

That morning became a pivotal point in my life
and in the entire corporate life of the congregation I serve. For as soon as I heard those words, I
rose from the bed, put on my bathrobe, and began to prayerfully ask the Lord to help me renew
the discipline of a daily, intimate, Holy Spirit-
sensitized walk with him.

Among the first things God did in response to

my prayer was to affirm his pleasure with what I had learned and done over the previous years. He let me know that he was pleased with the group prayer we had, which had become so vital and fulfilling in our church life; he affirmed the worship, praise, and thanksgiving that had recently become filled with a new understanding and responsiveness to a "Thy kingdom come" dimension of full-hearted worship; and he approved our intercessory prayer and spiritual warfare that had grown joyous and effective as we learned to apply principles of authority in spiritual conflict, and as we regularly witnessed genuine breakthrough in the circumstances and people that we prayed for.

But then he emphasized again that something had been forgotten: the daily discipline of being alone with Jesus at a personal, intimate level. That was the issue. God wasn't charging me with being prayerless or impersonal in my relationship with him, but he was letting me know that he wanted me to be renewed in a habit of disciplined, daily time with him—and with just him.

And, of course, I responded. You would, too. The very fact that you are reading these words indicates that you realize the importance of this issue. So it is a special joy to share with you what God taught me, and how he refreshed me, that morning and during the following season. Daybreak—the opening of each new day—became alive. Prayer became even more simply fulfilling; daily duties grew even more reflective of his wisdom. And, above all, I grew more consciously aware of his presence in all of my life.

Let me tell you how he began—how he brought me to his feet to look to him in a renewed way and to learn of him in a deeper way.

CHAPTER TWO
AT THE FEET OF JESUS

When we speak of a devotional exercise we must realize that devotions are not meant to be ritualistic or mystical. They are not intended to be so rigidly disciplined that they become cold rituals. Nor are they intended to be mysteriously romantic, as though intimacy in a spiritual relationship with Christ means being carried away into some trancelike experience.

Devotions are personal—very much so—and they involve coming to Jesus himself, in a direct, openhearted way, bowing humbly before the throne of God in worship, singing and presenting your whole being to your Creator. The practice of a devotional habit is a spiritual exercise, not just an intellectual one. It isn't a denial of your reasoning capabilities or a sensible thought process, but it is essentially a one-to-one relationship in the Spirit of God.

As such, the pursuit of a devotional walk with Jesus requires your openness to the Holy Spirit's searchings, stirrings, and surgings in and through your whole being—spirit, soul, and body.

THE PLACE TO START

Before you begin a practice of daily devotions, you need to learn the power of *coming to Jesus' feet*. As I said, that is where he drew me first after speaking to me about my need to be renewed in a devotional habit.

When this happened, I was reminded of Jesus' words which summarize the importance of the event recorded in Luke 10:38-42:

> As Jesus and the disciples continued on their way to Jerusalem they came to a village where a woman named Martha welcomed them into her home. Her sister Mary sat on the floor listening to Jesus as he talked.
>
> But Martha was the jittery type, and was worrying over the big dinner she was preparing. She came to Jesus and said, "Sir, doesn't it seem unfair to you that my sister just sits here while I do all the work? Tell her to come and help me."
>
> But the Lord said to her, "Martha, dear friend, you are so upset over all these details! There is really only one thing worth

being concerned about. Mary has discovered it—and I won't take it away from her!"

The words "only one thing worth being concerned about" struck me forcibly. They indicate
the *priority* of being with Jesus, personally and
devotionally. Then the phrase "on the floor,"
which reads "at Jesus' feet" in the New King
James Version of the Bible, stirred me and
captured my imagination. *Here*, I thought, *the
Word shows the exact place where I should bring
my devotion.*
As I reflected further on this passage, I became
impressed by the significance of someone being
at another person's feet. Such a position indicates
humility, teachableness, respect. Such a commitment to humbling yourself does not require or
imply a denial of your personhood; as though to
be "humble" means to renounce your identity.
Instead, true humility before God will lead you to
the realization of your true identity in Christ, and
to the renunciation of the substitute "identities"
we all tend to cultivate.
Whether we intend them or not, masks,
facades, and contrived behavior are too easily
generated and manifested in all of us. People and
pressures produce them. Certain habits or
life-styles develop that fail to reflect the true
person God created us to be. So the need for
discovering our true personhood—getting in
touch with the real you by coming to God—can
be powerfully life-restoring and releasing. And

this can only be found in his presence, at his feet.

As I read the surrounding passages in Luke, I noticed the frequency that those words, "at Jesus' feet," occurred. The same expression, or an equivalent, appears no fewer than nine times. And the more I meditated on those passages, the more I was shown how important it is for me to be in Christ's presence on a daily basis.

From this study, I discovered seven great blessings that can only be found "at Jesus' feet." We each need these blessings, these developments that will flow from our availability to be taught, to be touched, to be shaped.

1. SELF-DISCOVERY AND DIRECTION

> When Simon Peter realized what had happened, he fell to his knees before Jesus and said, "Oh, sir, please leave us—I'm too much of a sinner for you to have around." For he was awestruck by the size of their catch, as were the others with him, and his partners too—James and John, the sons of Zebedee.
>
> Jesus replied, "Don't be afraid! From now on you'll be fishing for the souls of men!" And as soon as they landed, they left everything and went with him. (Luke 5:8-11)

Peter's words "Leave us—I'm too much of a sinner" were not spoken by a newly repentant soul. Peter had recognized Jesus as Messiah well before this event occurred (see John 1). But here, when "he fell to his knees before Jesus" in the wake of the miracle, he was keenly aware of his need for deepened holiness.

In response to that hunger for more of God, Christ gave Peter new direction: "From now on you'll catch people—drawing them into my life!" The great principle emphasized in this passage is that the secret of discovering your life's meaning and purpose begins with Jesus. When we recognize who he is, we each recognize how much we need him, which then leads us to recognize what he created each of us to be and do.

2. PERSONAL HEALING AND RECOVERY

> One day in a certain village [Jesus] was visiting, there was a man with an advanced case of leprosy. When he saw Jesus he fell to the ground before him, face downward in the dust, begging to be healed.
>
> "Sir," he said, "if you only will, you can clear me of every trace of my disease."
>
> Jesus reached out and touched the man and said, "Of course I will. Be healed." And the leprosy left him instantly! Then Jesus instructed him to go at once without telling anyone what had happened and be examined by the Jewish priest. "Offer the sacrifice Moses' law requires for lepers who are healed," he said. "This will prove to everyone that you are well." (Luke 5:12-14)

By the simple action of falling on his face before Jesus, the leper speaks eloquently to us all. In his approach to the Savior, he symbolizes the fact that mankind's greatest affliction—our leprous bondage to pride, to "saving face"—is not solved by medical diagnosis and treatment. So the leper fell before the Lord Jesus, indicating not only his whole-hearted appeal for healing but also demonstrating the way to handle all of our sins: Casting them down, rejecting them completely.

The essence of sin is not so much in the action of sinning as it is in the source of sinning: Self-centeredness and fear-filled self-protection. When our fears seek to mask our inadequacies, pride takes over. Pretended self-sufficiency eventually leads to self-righteousness, and arrogance forces its rule of vanity as we grow to believe our own lies. But when we fall before Jesus, humbly and honestly, we can see our own "leprosy" healed.

For leprosy, that agonizing affliction of creeping decay in the members of a human body, has often been likened to the presence of sin in our human nature. And the healing of the leprous man, to whom Jesus responded so gently and willingly, holds a lesson for each of us who will come to his feet: There is nothing—personal weakness, inadequacy, failure, sinfulness—from which Christ cannot cleanse or deliver us. He is willing! He simply waits for us to cease trying to save our face, and seek his.

3. GRATEFUL WORSHIP AND ADORATION

> One of the Pharisees asked Jesus to come
> to his home for lunch and Jesus accepted
> the invitation. As they sat down to eat, a
> woman of the streets—a prostitute—heard
> he was there and brought an exquisite flask
> filled with expensive perfume. Going in,
> she knelt behind [Jesus] at his feet, weep-
> ing, with her tears falling down upon his
> feet; and she wiped them off with her hair
> and kissed them and poured the perfume
> on them. (Luke 7:36-38)

Few events in Scripture demonstrate tenderness
as does this passage. A woman who is despised
by the religionists of the day because of her
sinful past comes in humility to the table where
Jesus is dining with those who condemn her. She
shows Jesus an unabashed outpouring of devotion, sparing no expense even in the costly oint-
ment she applied to the Master's feet. She simply
doesn't seem to care what anyone thinks of her
love for Jesus! (Read verses 39-50.)

There is something here for us all to learn:
Coming to Jesus' feet in private prayer will have a
drastic affect on how we live our lives in public.
True worship at his feet will produce new values
in our lives, and we will become more concerned
about what God wills than what people want.

Further, just as this woman's deep appreciation

for the great forgiveness she received was demonstrated in her open adoration of the Savior, so our being at Jesus' feet has a way of enlarging our perspective on the greatness of our salvation. A healthy viewpoint of God's grace in our lives will increase our readiness to show our love for him no matter what the cost, and even when others are watching.

4. DELIVERANCE AND DISCIPLINED LIVING

So they arrived at the other side, in the Gerasene country across the lake from Galilee. As he [Jesus] was climbing out of the boat a man from the city of Gadara came to meet him, a man who had been demon-possessed for a long time. Homeless and naked, he lived in a cemetery among the tombs. As soon as he saw Jesus he shrieked and fell to the ground before him, screaming, "What do you want with me, Jesus, Son of God Most High? Please, I beg you, oh, don't torment me!"

For Jesus was already commanding the demon to leave him. This demon had often taken control of the man so that even when shackled with chains he simply broke them and rushed out into the desert, completely under the demon's power. "What is your name?" Jesus asked the demon. "Legion," they replied—for the man was filled with

thousands of them! They kept begging
Jesus not to order them into the Bottomless
Pit.

A herd of pigs was feeding on the mountainside nearby, and the demons pled with
him to let them enter into the pigs. And
Jesus said they could. So they left the man
and went into the pigs, and immediately the
whole herd rushed down the mountainside
and fell over a cliff into the lake below,
where they drowned. The herdsmen rushed
away to the nearby city, spreading the news
as they ran.

Soon a crowd came out to see for themselves what had happened and saw the man
who had been demon-possessed sitting
quietly at Jesus' feet, clothed and sane! And
the whole crowd was badly frightened.
(Luke 8:26-35)

The miracle of deliverance that Jesus worked in
the demoniac of Gadara is so dramatic, it may
seem without a parallel point in our lives. Yet
horrid and hellish workings of the Enemy's dark
powers are tormenting multitudes even today,
and deliverance is still available to those who
"fall to the ground before him."

The demoniac's first encounter at Jesus' feet
brought his deliverance, and freedom for any
oppression or bondage we may suffer is still
found before the Lord. However, an equally

instructive feature of this story is found in the
second time we see the man at Jesus' feet. Now
delivered, he is reported to be at Jesus' feet,
abiding there (v. 35). "Clothed and sane," he
models the way to live in the new path of freedom
in Christ. Deliverance gained in a moment is
made secure by maintaining a new life-style.

The Galatians were instructed, "So Christ has
made us free. Now make sure that you stay free
and don't get all tied up again in the chains of
slavery" (5:1). In the same way, we who have
come to Jesus need to learn not only the dynamic
of deliverance, but the disciplines of living in
that freedom. Continual freedom in life is sustained by being with Jesus . . . at his feet.

5. INTERCESSION AND FAMILY CONCERNS

> On the other side of the lake the crowds
> received him with open arms, for they had
> been waiting for him. And now a man
> named Jairus, a leader of a Jewish
> synagogue, came and fell down at Jesus'
> feet and begged him to come home with
> him, for his only child was dying, a little girl
> twelve years old. Jesus went with him,
> pushing through the crowds. (Luke 8:40-42)

Jairus's desperate appeal for Jesus to come to
his home and heal his dying daughter is filled
with the same emotion every thoughtful person
feels for his own family. Jairus makes his plea "at

Jesus' feet," and the Savior immediately responds.
Luke 8:49-56 relates the happy ending to the
story—an ending that the Holy Spirit would have
us all understand as more than simply history.
This episode is a prophecy for every parent,
every child, and every relative. This is an event
that demonstrates this promise: God answers the
prayers of people who come to Jesus' feet to
intercede for their loved ones.

Humanly speaking, Jairus's daughter's cir-
cumstance was futile. Still, just as Jairus came in
simple faith, let us do the same. There is no
situation so extreme, no death syndrome so
pronounced, that Jesus can't master it! Come to
his feet daily, believing that his saving power will
penetrate your whole family.

6. DRAINING AND DEFEATING SITUATIONS

> As they went a woman who wanted to be
> healed came up behind and touched
> [Jesus], for she had been slowly bleeding
> for twelve years, and could find no cure
> (though she had spent everything she had
> on doctors). But the instant she touched
> the edge of his robe, the bleeding stopped.
> "Who touched me?" Jesus asked.
> Everyone denied it, and Peter said,
> "Master, so many are crowding against
> you."
> But Jesus told him, "No, it was someone

who deliberately touched me, for I felt
healing power go out from me."

When the woman realized that Jesus
knew, she began to tremble and fell to her
knees before him and told why she had
touched him and that now she was well.

"Daughter," he said to her, "your faith has
healed you. Go in peace." (Luke 8:43-48)

How many people live a lifetime with one nag-
ging, wearying, draining problem plaguing them?
Too many precious saints—beloved children of
the Father—are deprived of life's fullest joy and
God's richest destiny for them because of such a
situation.

The woman who pressed her way through the
crowd was someone like this. But look! As she
risks being trampled by the mob she comes to
Jesus' feet and reaches for the fringe at the base
of his garment. Twelve years of unstanched
bleeding have left her weak, penniless, and still
afflicted. But she refuses to be kept from Jesus.

And there, at his feet, she is healed! Such a
healing often brings both a lesson and a promise.
The lesson is that no matter how long or hopeless
the plight—no matter how many human efforts
have been made to resolve it—you can bring it to
the feet of Jesus. And the promise is that Jesus'
power is still flowing outward, wherever and
whenever people reach to touch him. He is still
touched with our deepest needs (see Hebrews

4:15), so do not hesitate to reach out and express those needs to him.

7. VERIFICATION AND CONFIRMATION

And just as they were telling about it, Jesus himself was suddenly standing there among them, and greeted them. But the whole group was terribly frightened, thinking they were seeing a ghost!

"Why are you frightened?" he asked. "Why do you doubt that it is really I? Look at my hands! Look at my feet! You can see that it is I, myself! Touch me and make sure that I am not a ghost! For ghosts don't have bodies, as you see that I do!" As he spoke, he held out his hands for them to see [the marks of the nails], and showed them [the wounds in] his feet. Still they stood there undecided, filled with joy and doubt.

Then he asked them, "Do you have anything here to eat?"

They gave him a piece of broiled fish and he ate it as they watched! (Luke 24:36-43)

Into the panic-filled, upper-room hiding place, Jesus came to meet his disciples the evening following his resurrection. His approach shows the patience Jesus had with their fears, but it also shows how he aggressively presses the reality of his victory: he invites them to examine his wounds, now so completely and miraculously healed. "Handle me," he says, urging them to fellowship by taking his hands, and to worship by coming to his feet. And as they did this, the reality of his triumph was verified to them. They touched the tangible evidence of a resurrected, victorious Savior.

Thomas, who later heard of what had happened during his absence, would insist on the same right of verification, and he too was satisfied (see John 20:24-29). The witnesses of the resurrected Christ were not duped dummies. They were intelligent eyewitnesses of the greatest miracle and the surest fact in human history.

But the greatest factor of this miracle-fact is the confirmation it brings to us today: "Because I live, you too shall live!" (John 14:19, NKJV). These words of Jesus' tell you and me that if we will come to his feet, the Holy Spirit will cause the glorious reality of his resurrection victory to recharge our hearts with holy faith! People who live at the resurrected Lord's feet are never in doubt of his ultimate triumph in their lives. And so it was, as I studied these passages, that I was refreshed in the desirability of and the necessity for the "one thing worth being concerned about"—to be with Jesus, at his feet. These Scriptures warmed my heart with the wisdom of seeking him and the power of coming humbly and daily to his feet. Thus my quest began, to relearn that pathway to daily, devotional habit.

I knew Jesus wanted me to be with him in this way. And I knew that I wanted it too. And I could see that being in his presence and at his feet was the right way to begin a habit that would last the rest of my life.

CHAPTER THREE
A PATTERN FOR BEGINNING

As I considered the Lord's words to me, "You have forgotten the discipline of a daily devotional habit," I realized I was being summoned back to earlier years—to the first lessons I learned in devotion when an adolescent, standing on the brink of manhood.

I remember those mornings when, as a teen-ager, I knelt beside my bed and asked God's blessing on my day. I would simply talk with Jesus; praying for my parents, my brother and sister, my relatives, my school, and my own needs. I would read the Bible, noting simple truths that touched my heart and jotting down my thoughts in a small notebook. Between talking with the Lord and allowing his Word to talk to me, a relationship was being cultivated

that would support me through the coming years
of growth, development, and ministry.

Now I knew God was calling me to renew that
early simplicity. So in response to his call I
prayed: "Jesus, I am ready to learn again. Please
teach me anew." Just then the words Jesus spoke
in Revelation 2:4, 5, chiding those in the church at
Ephesus who lost their first love and offering
them a solution, flashed through my mind: "Turn
back to me again and work as you did before"
(v. 5). These words rekindled something inside
me. The truth was simple and clear: The way to
regain lost intimacy is to return to doing the
things you did when the simplicity and beauty of
that intimacy were fresh and alive.

It wasn't that I felt distant from God, but I felt
numb. I realized a new "feeling" wasn't the answer to everything, but I desired a definite,
renewed sense of Jesus' presence. And I knew he
was inviting me to a place where that "first love"
with him could be found again.

As he began to teach me, I began to jot down
notes, just as a teenage boy had done long ago. I
also wrote down simple references—verses that
everyone knew and that I had to force myself to
write out because they seemed so obvious that
I was tempted to bypass recording them. My
reward was the realization of the promise Jesus
gave to all of us in Matthew 18:3, when he says
that the rich dimensions of his kingdom will
open to those who are childlike in spirit. So it
was with me that day. His rule and reign began to

broaden and deepen within me, filling parts of
my soul that were thirstier than I realized.

Following is the pattern for beginning again
that Jesus gave me that day. His objective was to
help me relearn the basics of devotion—to meet
him at daybreak by (1) daily coming before the
Father's throne (see Psalm 24:3-6), (2) meeting
the Son at the Father's right hand (see Hebrews
1:3), and (3) reveling in the life of the Holy Spirit,
who is freely poured out into our hearts from
heaven (see Romans 5:5).

The outlined pattern that I will share with you
is intended to serve as a pathway, a roadmap that
points the way to arrive at a specific destination.
As with a map, there is no required pace for
covering the distance, nor can the whole picture
of the scenery along the way be shown. The
vision and beauty of all that can be seen as you
travel can only be experienced when the journey
is actually made.

So please begin now to focus on him, the
Savior to whom we make our approach. "Keep
your eyes on Jesus" (Hebrews 12:2) as you set
your course with patience. Make your objective
not so much to have a daily devotion as to be
with Jesus every day. When you take the time to
do this, you will find truth unfolding before you
like a magnificent panorama as you progress
along this pathway, following your Lord's guidance.

As you read this basic outline that helped me
back to a "first love" walk with Christ, you will

see that only one or two verses are given to
emphasize each point. Your own study in the
Bible will add many other verses to support the
truths contained here. The following three
chapters will explore the sections of this outline
in depth. But, to help you begin, here is an
overview of the steps to open your day with
Jesus, and experience the brightness of his kind
of daybreak.

STEP ONE: ENTERING HIS PRESENCE (THANKSGIVING AND PRAISE)

Begin by presenting yourself—your whole
being—to God (Mark 12:30).

A. You can find a new reason every day to do
this (Psalms 100:4; 118:24).

B. Present your body in worship to him
(Romans 12:1; Psalm 63:3, 4).

C. Sing a new song to the Lord (Psalm 96:1, 2;
Colossians 3:16).

D. Allow the Holy Spirit to assist your praise
(1 Corinthians 14:15; Jude 20).

STEP TWO: OPENING YOUR HEART (CONFESSION AND CLEANSING)

Present your heart to God and diligently seek
purity (Proverbs 4:23).

A. Invite the Lord to search your heart (Psalm
139:23, 24).

B. Recognize the danger of deception (Jeremiah 17:9; 1 John 1:6-10).

C. Set a monitor on your mouth and heart (Psalms 19:14; 49:3).

D. Keep Christ's purposes and goal in view (Psalm 90:12; Philippians 3:13, 14).

STEP THREE: ORDERING YOUR DAYS (OBEDIENCE)

Present your day, and submit to his ways and rule (1 Peter 5:6-11).

A. Surrender your day to God (Deuteronomy 33:25; Psalms 37:4, 5; 31:14, 15).

B. Indicate your dependence on him (Psalm 131:1-3; Proverbs 3:5-7).

C. Request specific direction for today (Psalm 25:4, 5; Isaiah 30:21).

D. Obey Jesus' explicit instructions (Matthew 6:11; 7:7, 8).

The outline came to me simply and readily after the Lord spoke to me that morning, and I knew a doorway was opening on something wonderfully fulfilling. I felt him. And I was receiving the blessing of his doing the same—drawing near to me.

CHAPTER FOUR
ENTERING HIS PRESENCE

What is the greatest expectation or anticipation you can remember experiencing? What was the occasion or event? Were you going to meet someone, or on a trip or visit? Where was it and who was going to be there?

Imagine a visit to the court of a king, the office of a president, or to the home of a dignitary. Or imagine one of these people coming to your home, and that he would be comfortable and unaffected in the ordinariness of your home, however plain or elaborate it may be.

Now, imagine daybreak with Jesus.

Think of the fact that he wants to be with you. Consider the possibility that a car would pull up to your home early each morning ... imagine you hear its door open and close, and then a quick knock sounds on your front door, announcing that Jesus is here to spend fifteen, twenty, even thirty minutes with you.

This situation is not only credible; it actually happens every day wherever Christ can find someone who will draw near to him. The Bible says: "Give yourselves humbly to God. Resist the devil and he will flee from you. And when you draw close to God, God will draw close to you" (James 4:7, 8).

This verse shows us that, although God is willing to draw close to each of us, there is a scriptural condition before he can do this: We must draw close to him first. He is fully ready, even warmly anxious, to respond to us—but he awaits invitation. It is not a matter of God needing some protocol to be observed, as though he were a cosmic prima donna or a hard-to-reach celebrity. He doesn't have the temperament for such human, contrived games. But he does know the human heart, and he knows that only those who will take the first step of faith and surrender themselves to him can really receive all he wants to give them.

Note that the Scripture verses from James give us two directives on "drawing near": submit and resist. Simply stated, the way to ensure an encounter with Jesus at daybreak—or at any other time, for that matter—is to submit yourself in obedient worship before the Father and to resist any distraction or discouragement that Satan may use to divert you. Both are necessary. We need to "draw near" by waking up, lifting our

praises to God, and countering any carnal or
spiritual hindrance to these actions.

I have found that the factors making up the
outline in the preceding chapter can serve as a
practical guide for drawing near to God. Let's
look at the elements of Step One more carefully.

STEP ONE: PRESENT YOURSELF TO HIM
In Mark 12:30, Jesus tells us, "You must love
[God] with all your heart and soul and mind and
strength." By these words, he helped us see that
the total human personality is summoned in
worship and devotion to God: the spirit (heart),
the emotions and will (soul), the intellect (mind),
and the body (strength). So approach the Lord in
exactly that way—enter his presence with your
total being!

> Go through his open gates with great
> thanksgiving; enter his courts with praise.
> Give thanks to him and bless his name. For
> the Lord is always good. He is always loving
> and kind, and his faithfulness goes on and
> on to each succeeding generation. (Psalm
> 100:4, 5)

Any approach to God involves worship. This
psalm calls for thanksgiving and praise, but
these actions sometimes have a way of dissolving
into the repetition of meaningless phrases. Many
of us too frequently just recite words, habitual if
not humdrum statements that begin well but

wear thin with overuse: "I thank you, Lord . . . I praise your name, O God . . . Hallelujah . . . Glory to God," and so on. Neither God nor man can fault the words, but thanks or praise will not last long or mean much without a specific point.

The Lord helped me in my renewal of a devotional habit by showing me a way to offer thanks and praise that keeps it current, expressive, and thoughtful.

FIND A NEW REASON EVERY DAY
TO THANK HIM.
This is the first element in Step One. I decided to begin each day by thanking God for some specific way that he had shown himself to me the day before. In other words, today's entry into God's presence becomes based on yesterday's evidence of his faithfulness. For example:

> Father, as I come before you today, I want to thank you for the way you helped me during that difficult conversation yesterday. The wisdom you gave me and the way it was resolved were wonderful indicators of your faithfulness. I thank you, Father.

With this thanksgiving for what has just happened, you will also find new avenues of praise to God for what is about to happen. You can anticipate experiencing something of himself and his ways today—with praise. I learned to do this by studying the different aspects of his

personality revealed in the various names the
Bible gives for God. Technically speaking, not all
of the terms are actually names, but they are
used to identify distinct traits and attributes of
God's personality. So each day I focused my
praise on a specific feature of God's own being.
This was especially meaningful when I focused
on a trait that met a need I had for that day:

> I praise you today, Father, for your *steadfast-
> ness*, the fact that you never change! I feel
> so slippery in my soul, Lord, and incapable
> of sustaining the attention needed to finish
> the work I know I have to get done today.
> Lord, pour your steadfastness into me and
> fill me so that I may stay firm until the
> work is done. I praise you, Lord, and lift my
> voice to exalt your greatness and your
> willingness to share yourself with me—to
> pour your fullness into my emptiness, your
> steadiness into my shakiness.

PRESENT YOUR BODY IN WORSHIP TO HIM.
This second element in Step One is both scriptural and practical. The Bible indicates that
worship is a physical act, as well as an intelligent
and spiritual one: "Give your bodies to God. Let
them be a living sacrifice" (Romans 12:1). David's
declaration that he would lift up his hands in
God's name (Psalm 63:3, 4) is but one of many
such statements in the Word of God. The body is
described in 1 Corinthians 6:19 as a living temple

of God's Holy Spirit, and as such it is obvious
that it was never meant to be passive in worship.

I have found it helpful to approach the Lord in
various postures and with different physical
expressions. If for no other reason (though this
may not seem particularly noble), I do this
because it helps me stay alert and awake on
those mornings when drowsiness could hinder
my daybreak appointment with the Lord. Oswald
J. Smith, the great missionary-statesman of the
past generation, admitted that he walked back
and forth during most of his daily quiet time with
God, and that a hidden benefit of doing this was
the defeat of lost concentration or dozing off.

Other physical worship expressions found in
Scripture include kneeling before Christ as your
Lord, lifting your hands unto God as your source,
standing in praise before your King, clapping
your hands with rejoicing, dancing with childlike
joy, bowing your head in humility, lifting your
head with expectancy, and prostrating yourself in
dependency.

Each of these postures expresses a stance of
the soul. You should take the time to do each of
them (though not all in one day, of course) and
consider what each physical position is reflecting
in a spiritual sense. For example, upraised hands
may express adoration, thankfulness, surrender,
hunger, or receptiveness. Kneeling may express
submission, obedience, and devotion. Each day,
you will find that the physical stance you use will
reflect a different feeling of your heart and

express in a different manner the hunger you
have for God.

SING A NEW SONG TO THE LORD.
Shouldn't every creature take part in this third
element of Step One, and sing at daybreak?

Of course. Yet, most of mankind is intimidated
into silence. Many of us compare our voices to
those more gifted in this area and conclude that
our voices aren't worthy to be lifted in song. But
God is not conducting a talent contest at our
private devotions! The same Creator who delights
in the singing of birds or the lowing of cattle on
the hillside waits to hear your song and mine.
But the Bible says to make it a "new song"
(Psalm 96:1, 2). How do we do that?

To begin, it can be encouraging to learn new
hymns and choruses as a part of your growth in
Christ. There is something to be said for expanding the number of worship songs you know.
Learning new music can help you avoid becoming
stale in your soul.

There is also a certain wisdom to be found in
an historic custom of each church member
carrying his own hymnal to and from church
gatherings, just as he did his Bible. This practice
contributed to the learning and understanding of
the enriching content of the lyrics. In fact, the
Bible directs you to "let [Christ's] words enrich
your lives and make you wise; teach them to each
other and sing them out in psalms and hymns

and spiritual songs, singing to the Lord with thankful hearts" (Colossians 3:16).

The Bible may also be used for singing. In William Law's *Serious Call to a Devout and Holy Life*, that eighteenth-century saint instructed every believer to open each morning by spontaneously singing or chanting one of the psalms. It's still a good idea and, of course, other Scripture may be sung as well. You may sing your own tunes or tunes that you've learned, but be sure of this: Whatever effort we make to sing praise to God in a "new song," he will hear and receive as a sweet sound to his ear.

> I will sing and give praise. Awake, my glory! Awake lute and harp! I will awaken the dawn. (Psalm 57:7, 8, NKJV)

ALLOW THE HOLY SPIRIT TO ASSIST YOUR PRAISE.

Worshipful singing often leads to the beautiful experience of Holy Spirit-assisted praise. Whether sung or spoken, this element is an appropriate part of our daily approach to the Lord.

> Don't drink too much wine, for many evils lie along that path; be filled instead with the Holy Spirit, and controlled by him. Talk with each other much about the Lord, quoting psalms and hymns and singing

sacred songs, making music in your hearts to the Lord. Always give thanks for everything to our God and Father in the name of our Lord Jesus Christ. (Ephesians 5:18-20)

Giving ourselves anew to the Spirit of God, inviting him to assist our worship in its energy and expression, is the quickest pathway to obeying the command to constantly keep filled with the Holy Spirit.

In 1 Corinthians 14:15, the Apostle Paul makes it clear that worship, praise, and thanksgiving are appropriate both in languages that are understood by the worshiper and in unknown languages that the Holy Spirit helps the worshiper speak. In that same chapter of Corinthians, Paul also gives careful controls concerning the use of such spiritual gifts in public services. But in our private devotions, we can take great freedom for practical, spiritual reasons.

There is an edifying quality to prayer and worship in the Holy Spirit. Paul found this to be so true that he was moved to gratefully acknowledge the fact that he had been able to use this form of prayer more than anyone else (see 1 Corinthians 14:18). What a powerful example he was for us to follow in our own daily devotional lives! In 1 Corinthians 14:15, Paul points the way to prayer empowered by the Holy Spirit, while setting forth a beautiful balance: "I will pray in unknown tongues and also in ordinary language that everyone understands. I will sing in unknown tongues and also in ordinary language, so that I can understand the praise I am giving."

Praying with the Spirit "in unknown tongues" is not to be used to the exclusion of our praying "in ordinary language that everyone understands." It is not a substitute form of prayer but a complementing form. In fact, the Bible seems to suggest that Holy Spirit-assisted prayer often can help us pray better, more effective prayers in our known language. It is as if our minds are washed and cleared, aided to think and pray more clearly in line with God's will and purpose (see Romans 8:26, 27).

So we are wise to heed Paul's words of balance as we come to God, with our singing and our praying being expanded by the Holy Spirit as he enlarges our expressions of love to the Lord Jesus and of worship to the eternal Father.

These, then, are the four elements of entering the Lord's presence and drawing near to him:

- Thanksgiving and prayer are offered thoughtfully.
- The temple of your body is presented physically.
- Your voice is lifted in a new song creatively.
- Praise is assisted by the Holy Spirit beautifully.

This first set of stepping-stones marks the beginning of a pathway to a daily devotional habit—a regular meeting with Jesus at daybreak. This beginning doesn't need to take a lot of time; it could be completed in a matter of three or four

•

minutes. But there will be times when you find the moments flying by and you will linger in worship, singing, and presenting your total self to him.

It's important to realize that the amount of time you take for this exercise probably will be different each day. Don't let the beauty of an openhearted spontaneity be spoiled by a self-imposed time schedule. God isn't calling you to punch in on a heavenly time clock. He simply calls you to draw near to him, assuring you that when you do so, he'll be there.

CHAPTER FIVE
OPENING YOUR HEART

There is no more intricate or crucial part of the human makeup than that part of the personality we call the "heart." The importance of our spiritual "heart" to our health and survival is parallel to the importance of our physical heart. Without a healthy physical heart, every other function of the body is diminished, and so it is with the heart of our "inner man."

The Bible tells us that we need to be sensitive, guarding our heart attitudes (see Proverbs 4:23); to remember that God judges men in view of what's in their hearts (see 1 Samuel 16:7); that wisdom and revelation are keys to gaining an understanding heart (see Ephesians 1:17, 18); and that God is searching for people whose hearts desire him and his ways (see 2 Chronicles 16:9).

Several times in the Bible we are urged to be pure of heart, to have a heart that is uncluttered by accumulated attitudes that are inconsistent with God's heart and purposes. A pure heart is undiluted by confusing mixtures of motives or secret reservations. Purity of heart doesn't mean a person has arrived at perfection, but it does mean that there is only one direction in his life: following Jesus!

STEP TWO: PRESENT YOUR HEART TO GOD

Daybreak is the time to meet Jesus for a daily heart checkup. This part of your daily devotions isn't intended to prompt a paranoid self-examination or a wearying preoccupation with self-holiness. Neither the church nor God needs (or wants) a bunch of self-righteous prudes or nit-picking Pharisees. But it is a time to deal with the fact that because we are human our souls are too easily clouded through the pollution of our hearts. Gaining a clear vision of the Father's face and a pure perspective on his will in our lives are dimmed if our hearts aren't carefully guarded.

Proverbs 4:23 says: "Keep your heart with all diligence, for out of it spring the issues of life" (NKJV). The elements of Step Two in the outline I presented give us some suggestions for "keeping our hearts." Using these suggestions we can present our hearts to the Lord daily, obediently keeping them "with all diligence."

INVITE THE LORD TO SEARCH YOUR HEART.
No one in the Bible understands the heart's place
in one's relationship with God better than David
(see 1 Samuel 13:14). Beyond his failings and
beside his victories, David's earnest desire to
walk before God with his whole heart is an
unsurpassed example of what pleases God the
most. David demonstrated a practical point of
wisdom for us when he prayed, "Search me, O
God, and know my heart; test my thoughts. Point
out anything you find in me that makes you sad,
and lead me along the path of everlasting life"
(Psalm 139:23, 24).

David's "open door policy" toward God teaches
us a fundamental lesson: The purpose of having
God search our hearts is so we may discover
sin and confess it. This kind of openness—
confessing sin without self-justifying debate—allows the Lord free entry to examine and correct
us. We accept his dealings and agree with his
assessments.

When I was a boy, each Saturday my father
would make a list of chores for me to do before I
could go and play. When he came home in the
evening, he would take the list and—walking
with me beside him—check how each job had
been done. Sometimes he would point out a
hidden, unswept corner that I had missed or find
a small, untrimmed area of the yard that I had
overlooked. When he did so, I would take a brush
or clippers right then and finish the job properly.

And you can be sure that, the next week, I would remember to carefully check those places I'd missed.

In checking on my work, my father was not being unkind or critical of what I'd done. He was helping me learn to do a job right the first time. And when I did, he would always encourage me and say, "That's good work, son."

That's how we should be with the Lord. We need to learn to be quick to take care of everything we see on the Father's "list" in his Word and then be open and ready for him to point out the things we have overlooked or neglected. We must offer daily confession, both for known sins that blot a day's activities and for sins we overlooked.

When we do these things, we know that through the blood of Christ we have instant and complete forgiveness: "If we confess our sins to him, he can be depended on to forgive us and to cleanse us from every wrong" (1 John 1:9).

"Hidden corners" do slip by unnoticed, and there are many believers caught up in sinful habits that at first they don't even recognize as sin. We might find, as we open to the Lord, that he begins to confront and adjust a pattern of our relationships, an aspect of our daily activities or entertainment, or some continued practice from childhood. We need to bring all aspects of our lives, regardless of what the world says is right or acceptable, under the searching eyes of the Lord.

As a pastor, I spend a great deal of time trying

to help people who are struggling with problems caused by "hidden corners"—behavioral and thought patterns that came from their early life, often before they met the Lord. The core of a present difficulty frequently stems from doing or saying things that a person hasn't come to recognize as wrong. And, because salvation is comprehensive and instant, some people don't realize that they need to grow and change.

No sincere believer determines to turn his back on God's wisdom and stubbornly sin; yet many sincere people fumble on, continuing ignorantly and far too long in regular patterns of sinning. Usually they end up hurt, wounded inside because they didn't learn to walk daily with Jesus, to wait in his presence and listen to his guiding voice.

If we will only listen, he will teach us and refine our walk along the pathway of purity. But we must come with an open heart, ready to listen and to let the Father "check up" on our daily words and actions. And daybreak is the best starting point for this checkup. Learning to invite the Lord's searching of our hearts can protect us from many future problems. When we abandon ourselves—our thoughts, motives, ambitions, and plans—to God's scrutiny, we become open to receiving his leading in every decision of our lives, no matter how great or small.

So swing wide the doors of your heart! Like David, say, "God, come walk the corridors of my being. Search me, examine me, bring my 'hidden

corners' into your light!" When you ask God to
reveal your unrecognized sins, he will lovingly
respond to you and sweep every corner clean.

And as you listen to him through the day, you
will hear his voice when night comes saying,
"That was a good job, my child. I'm really proud
of you."

RECOGNIZE THE DANGER OF DECEPTION.
Deception is believing something is right when it
is wrong. The prophet Jeremiah warned that the
human heart is full of deceit: "The heart is the
most deceitful thing there is" (Jeremiah 17:9).
This is why we must bring our hearts under
God's review every day. We are too quick to
suppose we are right in our actions, analyses of
situations, or opinions of people.

The fact that most people sincerely think they
are right is at the core of most human error and
misunderstanding. But sincerity doesn't prevent
deception. Our sincerity, regardless of how
powerful it may be, cannot overcome the fundamental weakness sin brings to our nature.
Charlie Brown says of his baseball team, "How
can we lose when we're so sincere?" But lose
they do, and likewise many sincere people lose
sight of God's way of victory, drifting into deception without recognizing how off-target they have
become.

But if the heart is opened to God, and we
acknowledge our ability to be deceived before
God, something wonderful happens. When we

humbly and daily admit our need for Christ's teaching, correction, and forgiveness, he will respond to us and help us past deception's blind spots.

For example, suppose I feel sorely misunderstood by someone who has said something that hurt my feelings—something unkind or hostile toward me. The situation might seem so clear, the person's hostility so pronounced, that I believe it to be my right to come to the Lord for justice—expecting him, obviously, to side with me. Imagine my surprise when I discover that, because he knows not only my heart but the heart of the other person involved, God doesn't see the situation as I do. A much better attitude for me would be to come to God with a teachable, correctable heart and to ask the Lord for instructions on understanding the situation as it really is.

God ministers to every individual with a perfect knowledge of each person's needs. While he will certainly understand my hurt feelings and comfort me when I have been mistreated, he will also be concerned with all that is happening to and in the other person. I may consider that other person my adversary, but Jesus cares as much about that person's needs as he does about mine. And he wants me to learn this and open my heart to being used by him to bridge rifts in relationships.

The only way to reconciliation in broken relationships is for one person to initiate the restoration by showing his understanding of the other person's fears, his past, and his pain. None of us by nature is inclined to accept that responsibility, so we each need to develop a special openness of heart. We need to refuse the temptation to argue our own cases and see beyond the deception that our perception of the situation must be right.

Coming before the Lord with an open heart will help us overcome the temptations of self-defensiveness and insensitivity to others, and will help prevent bitterness or resentment from finding a harbor within us.

Another kind of deception comes in the guise of opportunity. Opportunities may appear beneficial to our position, but sometimes people make serious mistakes by walking through the open doors of an apparent opportunity without consulting the Lord. Sometimes we presume that, since we have taken some steps with God's blessing, all our steps will receive that same blessing. But yesterday's wisdom doesn't insure that we won't walk in foolishness today. We must open our hearts to receive his teaching and correction each and every day.

Israel's early victories in Canaan under Joshua's leadership were won with God's direction and help. But they became an ironic occasion of deception for the men of Gibeon who forged a treaty with Israel under false pretenses (read Joshua 9). Why did Joshua and his men find themselves in such a tangle? "They did not bother to ask the Lord" (v. 14).

So let's learn these lessons: (1) we aren't always right; (2) people who hurt us aren't always wrong; and (3) opportunities are not necessarily God-ordained and should always be handled with prayer. Our hearts' ability to deceive us into sin and into being insensitive toward others and opportunistic in our approach to life can only be held in check when we accept the warning of Scripture and seek the counsel of the Lord.

SET A MONITOR ON YOUR MOUTH AND HEART.

According to Jesus, "A man's heart determines his speech" (Matthew 12:34). The importance of this truth in our daily lives is better understood in view of the relationship between the heart and the mouth, both positive and negative, as shown in Scripture.

Positive Relationship.

1. In our salvation: "For if you tell others with your own mouth that Jesus Christ is your Lord, and believe in your own heart that God has raised him from the dead, you will be saved" (Romans 10:9).

2. In exercising our faith: "In reply Jesus said to the disciples, 'If you only have faith in God— this is the absolute truth—you can say to this Mount of Olives, "Rise up and fall into the Mediterranean," and your command will be

obeyed. All that's required is that you really
believe and have no doubt!' " (Mark 11:22, 23).

Negative Relationship.
   1. In compromising integrity: "Pretty words
may hide a wicked heart, just as a pretty glaze
covers a common clay pot" (Proverbs 26:23).
   2. In expressing anger and deceit: "And by all
means don't brag about being wise and good if
you are bitter and jealous and selfish; that is the
worst sort of lie. For jealousy and selfishness
are not God's kind of wisdom. Such things are
earthly, unspiritual, inspired by the devil" (James
3:14, 15).

When you consider this strong connection
between the heart and the mouth—how the
inner heart can inspire words that either save,
heal, and bless or that destroy, injure, and curse—
it's no wonder that the psalmist prayed:

> May my spoken words and unspoken
> thoughts be pleasing even to you, O Lord
> my Rock and my Redeemer. (Psalm 19:14)

The best way to apply the wisdom of this
prayer at daybreak is to take two steps: Test the
day behind you, and then offer God the day
ahead of you.

First, review with Jesus any of yesterday's
conversations or comments. Is there anything
that he brings to your mind for consideration?
Was there a slip of the tongue that needs to be

confessed in prayer? Or was there a wrong attitude of heart—were you feeling bitter, proud, or angry? These "spoken words and unspoken thoughts" are at the source or the fountainhead of our living, and there is no better way to keep the fountain of our lips and deeds pure than to have the fountainhead checked daily by the Master.

Second, place the upcoming day's encounters before the Lord. Ask him to post the Holy Spirit as a guard at the doorway of your mouth. Open yourself so that you may hear him cautioning or signaling you when your thoughts aren't right and when you are about to speak cutting or unwise words.

There is a reward for such an open heart and attitude before God; a God-given answer to the prayer that our words and thoughts might be acceptable to him. This is summarized in Psalm 49:3:

> My mouth shall speak wisdom, and the
> meditation of my heart shall bring under-
> standing. (NKJV)

What a promise!

KEEP CHRIST'S PURPOSES AND GOAL IN VIEW.

God's purpose in calling us to purity—in teaching us to examine our hearts, bare our souls, confess our sins, and receive his cleansing—must always be kept in view. God does not seek holiness for holiness's sake. He is not in the business of making people clean so that he can put them on pedestals like plaster images. Instead, he calls us to holiness for an entirely practical reason. The goal of a day-by-day quest for a perfect heart, wise actions, and sensitive speech is to make every day of our lives worthwhile.

Psalm 90:12 says, "So teach us to number our days that we may gain a heart of wisdom" (NKJV). This "wisdom" is knowing the right thing to do at the right time. That kind of living is the outward goal of our seeking holiness. Daily reviewing of our lives and our living at Jesus' feet is the means to wholesome, healthy, fruitful work and relationships. And that's the goal of holiness: well-rounded, fulfilling, workable living.

But God also has an inward purpose for drawing us toward a holy life; a personal goal for each of us to share with him.

> And we know that all that happens to us is working for our good if we love God and are fitting into his plans. For from the very beginning God decided that those who came to him—and all along he knew who would—should become like his Son, so that his Son would be the First, with many brothers. (Romans 8:28, 29)

These words from Romans are quoted frequently because they are a source of comfort in difficult or trying times. But four important words are often overlooked: "fitting into his plans." They point to the fact that God's ultimate loving objective for every believer's life is that he becomes like his Son, Jesus.

God calls us to this warmly and lovingly, and our response to him needs to be "Do this, Lord. Make us like Jesus, like yourself."

So the main goal of all our "heart-keeping"—of being at Jesus' feet when we meet with him daily at daybreak—is to become like him. When we ask him to search the corridors of our lives, it isn't merely to have them swept clean but to rid us of anything that hinders his image being revealed in each of us. Becoming alert to the danger of deception is not simply a quest for being right, but a quest to allow his liberating truth-fullness to overflow our lives and make us and others free. And asking the Holy Spirit to guard our mouths and our hearts isn't an exercise born of fear, but a request based on the desire for the Wisdom of God—Jesus Christ—to be seen in our lives!

This is the goal of a daily walk with Jesus. In understanding this, we can see that the quest for purity and holiness moves from the realm of ritual to the realm of practicality. And when we grasp this practical dynamic of our walk, our pressing forward to develop this devotional habit will take on the dimensions described by the Apostle Paul in Philippians 3:13, 14:

No, dear brothers, I am still not all I should
be but I am bringing all my energies to bear
on this one thing: Forgetting the past and
looking forward to what lies ahead, I strain
to reach the end of the race and receive the
prize for which God is calling us up to
heaven because of what Christ Jesus did
for us.

That verse became one of my favorites when I
was only fourteen years old. Esther Kerr Rusthoi,
the beloved evangelist/hymn writer, was preach-
ing at our church in Oakland, California. In one
message, she related the story of a close brush
with death when she and several others were
trapped in a dry riverbed just as a flash flood hit.
As the rushing waters rose rapidly, the people in the group joined hands and pressed
against the mounting flood. By standing together,
they were able to avoid being swept downstream,
and they eventually made their way to safety.

Her story, used to illustrate the text above,
moved my young heart deeply. I vividly remember
my heart's response to the Lord that night: "That
is the kind of person I want to be. I want to 'press
on' against the stream of this world, and gain the
very best you have for my life in Christ."

And that verse still expresses my long-range
goal, my life's purpose in the Lord. But I now
know that long-range goals are only achieved
through completing a series of daily short-range

goals—and beginning each day with Jesus is the most worthwhile, practical short-range goal we can set.

So let us press on together, at daybreak, realizing that as our daily goals are achieved, the long-range ones become easily attainable.

CHAPTER SIX
ORDERING YOUR DAYS

It was the night before Christmas and I had just opened a large box containing what seemed to be a thousand pieces of metal, precut to be assembled into a toy gas station—a present Anna and I had bought for our two sons. I scooped aside the smaller pieces—the cars, gas pumps, and trucks—figuring that if I didn't get them put together in time the boys would enjoy doing so later. But I wanted the main feature, the gas station itself, completed.

The larger pieces, fifteen or twenty in all, were fairly easy to identify from the picture on the front of the box. I gave them my attention, believing they could be assembled quickly since the structural design was fairly obvious. There could be only one way to put them together . . . or so it seemed.

Disregarding the box's clearly written instructions of "Do not assemble without reading directions," I proceeded to fasten several of the major pieces together, reasonably certain the directions would only be important when I came to the smaller pieces. I was anxious to get something done, to take a sizeable bite out of the project and be sure something substantial was ready to be displayed under the tree.

Then I came to the piece that wouldn't fit anywhere.

I looked at the picture again and could see clearly where it was supposed to go. But none of the metal fastening clips that extended from the small wall I held in my hand would align with the slots in the toy's floor. I was about to decide there was something faulty in the toy's design, frowning with the disappointment of not having the gift ready, when it occurred to me to look at the directions.

Need I go on? Suffice it to say that I had put everything together precisely backward! What had seemed so simple and obvious, wasn't really that simple after all. For the next half-hour I dismantled what I had assembled, undoing one clip after another until I was back to the original pile of pieces. Then, following the directions, I was able to accomplish my task and present my boys with the assembled toy.

This was a valuable lesson on one of life's

major principles: The practical wisdom of submission. I don't think I've ever understood
submission more clearly than I did with that toy
gas station.

STEP THREE: SUBMITTING YOUR
LIFE TO GOD

Submission essentially has to do with order, with
intended design and right relationship. While the
idea of submitting often seems to be twisted to
refer to dominating people and reducing them to
servile obedience, in reality it refers to things
being in proper arrangement so that they will
work properly. The toy gas station demonstrated
this: When I "submitted" to the directions, all the
pieces fit. When I thought I could figure it out on
my own, they didn't.

The final step, Step Three, of the outline to
fruitful fellowship with Jesus at each day's
daybreak brings us to a realization: Our days—
the pieces of time that constitute our lives—need
to be submitted. On one hand, we have the
smaller pieces of hours, minutes, and seconds;
on the other hand, we have the larger pieces of
weeks, months, and years. And midway in the
chronological components of our lives is that
structural segment we call "today." Often, those
twenty-four hours—1440 minutes or 86,400
seconds—make it seem a rather large segment
and tempt us to think we can "fit it together"
without help, as I mistakenly assumed I could fit

the toy together without the directions. However, we must realize that our days "fit" better when they are submitted to God for his guidance, so that he may arrange them in the proper order, and we avoid having to dismantle our efforts and start all over again.

THE VALUE OF A DAY

The Bible is pointed about the value of each individual day and is equally direct in speaking of our responsibility to use these pieces of time wisely and profitably:

- We are to consider each day a valuable gift, and look to God for wisdom in using that gift. "Teach us to number our days and recognize how few they are; help us to spend them as we should" (Psalm 90:12).
- We are to treat each day separately, recognizing that "one day at a time" isn't just a clever slogan but is a practical guideline to help us stay sensitive to today's duties and not worry about tomorrow. "So don't be anxious about tomorrow. God will take care of your tomorrow too. Live one day at a time" (Matthew 6:34).
- We are specifically directed to use prayer and God's Word each day; our personal provision and success are directly dependent upon our doing so. "Constantly remind the people about these laws, and you yourself must think about them every day and every

night so that you will be sure to obey all of them. For only then will you succeed" (Joshua 1:8).

We are promised strength for living on a daily basis, and we are shown that personal guidance also is best sought daily. "Show me the path where I should go, O Lord; point out the right road for me to walk. Lead me, teach me; for you are the God who gives me salvation. I have no hope except in you" (Psalm 25:4, 5). This simple collection of scriptural truth concerning our responsible use of each day is enough to encourage us to break the sloppiness of thought which characterizes most of our culture. The average person doesn't believe he is accountable for his use of time, except perhaps to his employer. Our days are too readily viewed as disposable; accountability is disregarded and time is squandered. But the earnest believer will come to each day's beginning—to daybreak—with the dual sense of joy and sobriety: joy at receiving the gift of another day, and sobriety at recognizing that he is accountable to the Lord for how he will spend that day.

"Today" is always bright with promise and weighed down with duty; it is as easy to spend it profitably as it is to waste it. How wise it is, then, to bring each day to the Lord, to ask his guidance in its intended purpose and its best use. This is the purpose of Step Three in the outline: presenting your day to the Lord. When you take this step,

you will find your daybreak appointment with
God turning a corner.

Steps One and Two of the outline focus on
your being, on what you are. And they emphasize
your relationship with Jesus, calling you to be
honest and intimate with him while being candid
and confrontational with yourself as you come to
him.

But with this third step, the focus turns to
what you do, to the things that you are responsible for every day. You must learn to systemati-
cally and personally present the details of each
day to the Lord in prayer; to acknowledge him as
your Lord and Master at the beginning of each
day. He will never force his way into your day or
just take over your daily business. His wisdom
and provision for all of your life and day are
easily available when you ask for them.

> If you want to know what God wants you to
> do, ask him, and he will gladly tell you, for
> he is always ready to give a bountiful
> supply of wisdom to all who ask him; he
> will not resent it. (James 1:5)

Presenting your day to God is the key to
receiving his blessing and wisdom for all the day
will contain. We need that. We all need to know
what God wants us to do, for we all lack wisdom.
So let's establish a habit of asking him for daily
direction, thereby establishing a close partner-

ship with Jesus that begins, each day, with our
daybreak meetings.

To learn how to present your day to God, let's
take a look at the individual elements of Step
Three.

SURRENDER YOUR DAY TO GOD.

Years ago I began a practice that I still observe
nearly every morning. Instead of getting out of
bed by sitting up and standing, I slide my feet and
legs over the edge of the bed and kneel at my
bedside. I don't consider this so much a prayer
time as a moment of commitment, for this is
when I say, "Lord Jesus, for this day I again
declare that you are my Lord. I submit this day
and all it contains to you."

That's it.

I get up from my knees, having been there for
fewer than ten seconds, and I go into my day.
Several minutes later I will come to meet the
Lord for a more extensive time as my daybreak
appointment takes place, but in those first few
seconds of the day I believe I am responding to
the psalmist's directive:

> Commit everything you do to the Lord.
> Trust him to help you do it and he will. Your
> innocence will be clear to everyone. He will
> vindicate you with the blazing light of
> justice shining down as from the noonday
> sun. (Psalm 37:5, 6)

Note the words "with the blazing light" and "from the noonday sun." They signal a promise: The simple action of committing your day is a guarantee of blessing. The Lord's increasing brightness will fill your days until every shadow is gone! Just as irresistibly as the sun rises and masters the darkness, our Lord will bring the effects of his loving purpose into our daily lives.

When you commit your day to Jesus, you surrender it. You acknowledge the words of Psalm 31:14, 15: "You alone are my God; my times are in your hands." In these words, we see that the Father distributes to us our hours and days, as well as the strength and blessing we need to face the trials and challenges we will encounter. "As your days, so shall your strength be," he promises in Deuteronomy 33:25 (NKJV). He has promised us his personal, attentive concern for each demand in every day.

INDICATE YOUR DEPENDENCE ON HIM.
God's Word also calls us to daily dependence upon God. But our perspective on this idea must be balanced so that no one thinks God is seeking to cultivate a band of groveling serfs. Never! Rather, he is wanting to grow a family of sons and daughters who are partners with him.

When the Bible teaches us to come to him dependently, the image is not that of infantile or simpering behavior but of children coming to a loving Father. The real meaning of this kind of dependence can be seen in David. Though he was a bold warrior and a dynamic political leader, he still described the attitude of his heart before God in humble terms: "I am quiet now before the Lord, just as a child who is weaned from the breast" (Psalm 131:2). In saying this he revealed that he understood that, before God, he was a child who was quietly dependent on his parent. Yet, though a child, he refused to act like a whimpering baby, whining for attention.

In the same passage, David declares, "Lord, I am not proud and haughty. I don't think myself better than others. I don't pretend to 'know it all' " (v. 1). These two sections of this psalm frame a delicate and beautiful balance for our understanding of humble dependence. Here is a man of achievement, of leadership skills and creative accomplishments, who is saying, "God, I know so little and need you so much!" Such humility and acknowledged dependence on the Lord do not come easily, but the desire and quest to learn them are important parts of the daybreak pathway.

Every one of us struggles with the desire for independence. Many of us tend to think that God is only to be turned to in times of crisis. The rationale for this deception goes something like this: "Generally, for most matters of life, we're alone and responsible. God gave us brains to think with and bodies to work with, so it's up to us—God helps those who help themselves."

There is a smattering of truth in this statement,

for God did give us brains and bodies to use. But this isn't enough to veil its error-filled vanity or arrogant self-sufficiency. The real, whole truth is this: You and I need the Lord's help every second, every minute, every day. Acknowledging our honest dependency is not resigning our own responsibilities, but it is the most logical stance a creature can take. We have been made by him, and we must be sustained by him.

The benefit of living in such an understanding—that God is your Source and you are his son or daughter—is guaranteed fruitfulness:

> I am the Vine; you are the branches. Whoever lives in me and I in him shall produce a large crop of fruit. For apart from me you can't do a thing. . . . If you stay in me and obey my commands, you may ask any request you like, and it will be granted! My true disciples produce bountiful harvests. (John 15: 5-8)

REQUEST SPECIFIC DIRECTION FOR TODAY. "In everything you do, put God first, and he will direct you. . . ." That's what it means to request specific direction from the Lord. Solomon calls us to act on this wisdom each day, for each part of that day. To really understand what it is to request direction, study the following verses:

> Trust the Lord completely; don't ever trust yourself. In everything you do, put

God first, and he will direct you and crown your efforts with success. Don't be conceited, sure of your own wisdom. Instead trust and reverence the Lord, and turn your back on evil. (Proverbs 3:5-7)

The wisdom of this text from God's Word gives us a threefold directive:

1. "Don't be conceited, sure of your own wisdom." Don't suppose that because of your experience or expertise that you know the answers to the questions you will face today. The Bible strictly warns against thinking you can easily accomplish today's duties without presenting them in prayer to the Lord.

2. "In everything you do, put God first." Take time in counsel with the Lord, allowing him to help you outline the basic tasks and responsibilities your day holds. As you do this, you will find an order coming into your day. Whatever you put in the Lord's hands will always return with his blessing!

3. "He will direct you." This is God's promise and he will keep it. Through this verse he is saying, "If you acknowledge me, I'll take control of your day in a way that will assist and profit you." He is not saying he will turn us into robots, directing our paths by some push-button, computerized operation in heaven, but that he will lead us through every detail of each day.

A Wedding Day Surprise. Recently I was outlining the day before the Lord. At one point, I said something like this: "And Lord, please bless Anna and me as we go to the wedding this afternoon, and make it a special day for our friends who are being wed."

This was only a portion of what was neither a profound or lengthy prayer. But what happened at the wedding assured me that the results of reciting your day's expected agenda to Jesus at daybreak are ceaselessly surprising. At 2:00 that afternoon, Anna and I arrived at the church where the wedding was to be held. As we walked toward the building, I remembered something I needed from the car. Explaining this to my wife, I told her, "You go ahead, honey. I'll be there in just a minute." She knew many of the guests, so she didn't mind this and proceeded through the line to sign the guest book.

I went to my car and, just as I was closing the door again, a picture flashed through my mind: I saw myself greeting the bride in the church Bride's Room. I recognized this as the Holy Spirit's way of directing me, so—because I have learned to respond to such promptings—I walked back toward the church sure that I had a brief mission to fulfill. Since I was familiar both with the church and with the family and friends of the wedding party, I made my way easily to the appropriate room where I knocked on the door and announced myself.

The bride and bridesmaids had finished their preparations and were waiting to be called to the processional, so the bride's mother invited me directly into the room. The bridesmaids were all beautiful, but especially moving was the bride's face when she saw me. She quickly came to meet me, smiling brightly, her eyes brimming with tears of joy. There was something very, very special about my making this brief prewedding visit, for God had allowed me to help this girl through a deep difficulty in her life some years before. And in an unusual way, my stopping in to see her on this special day spoke volumes to her. She not only sensed my affirmation, but she felt God's loving assurance.

To anyone else, the whole episode could have passed without notice. But Jesus caused something quite powerful to take place in that young bride's heart. Neither my plan nor foresight prompted the occurrence. It was Christ who handed me a special moment to minister something of his love and life to one of his children. It was a peculiarly important and wonderful wedding gift from Jesus' heart to the bride's heart, and I knew she was as aware of this as I was.

Christ had arranged for his touch to be on this girl in a tender way as she prepared to walk down a rose-strewn aisle to exchange vows with the dearest man in her life. Somehow, the Lord let me stand in for him for just a minute, as though to say to her, "Everything in your wounded past is sealed closed, and everything of your tomorrows is as open and bright as my promises!" My whole point in telling this story is that I'm sure the blessing wouldn't have taken place if I hadn't opened myself to the Spirit's prompting by asking for specific direction that morning. Through that request, I knew I was open to whatever God would ask of me.

Of course, I don't look for special things like this to happen all the time, as though spiritual living requires us to try hard to make something wonderful happen every day. In fact, I am uneasy when people seem obliged to interpret everything that happens as some phenomenal, miraculous happening, or feel constrained to help God along by imposing themselves on others in the name of "being spiritual." But Jesus Christ does lead those who ask him to do so, and he does give promptings through the Holy Spirit. And since Jesus dearly loves us, he will use us to touch others in his name; leading us by his Spirit in various ways to touch them with his love.

Jesus does work miracles—great and mighty ones—but he also does small, special ones as he did that day in a church's Bride's Room. So let me encourage you to take the following two passages very seriously as you come to meet Christ each morning:

> Show the path where I should go, O Lord; point out the right road for me to walk. Lead me; teach me; for you are the God who gives me salvation. I have no hope except in you. (Psalm 25:4, 5)
> And if you leave God's paths and go

> astray, you will hear a Voice behind you say, "No, this is the way; walk here." (Isaiah 30:21)

These verses very clearly teach that we can ask God for specific direction for the day, and that we can expect him to give us that direction at crucial points if we will only stay open to him. And, though God doesn't want us to become mystical or superstitious, we can expect Jesus to direct us in ways that are custom-made, especially designed to bless others and us in the process.

Isaiah 30:21, noted above, is God's promise to help us avoid serious mistakes or errors. Thus we can confidently know that he will lead us down pathways of blessing as well as keep us going on the path of practical, good-sense living with him.

Speaking of good sense, when teaching people to expect God's leading in daily details it seems sadly inevitable that someone will make a foolish or fanatical application of this truth. Imagine someone stopping his car at every corner while driving, waiting and praying to be shown which way to turn. Such exaggerated practices and applications are superstitious, not spiritual. But our Savior is very sensible, practical, and gentlemanly. He isn't weird, nor does he call us to weird behavior. As you come to know him better through your daybreak meetings, you will discover that his truths are meant to bless your life, not confuse it.

OBEY JESUS' EXPLICIT INSTRUCTIONS.
In the Lord's Prayer, Jesus taught us to pray,
"Give us this day our daily bread." That prayer is
precise and powerful in its implicatons. First, by
its very definition, it directs daily prayer for our
basic supply of resources. Second, Jesus em-
phasizes more than our need for bread; he's
pointing out our need to ask.

"Ask, and you will be given what you ask for,"
he says in Matthew 7:7. The obvious directive to
pray somehow seems to cloud our understanding
this as more than merely a matter of request.
James issues the warning, "The reason you don't
have what you want is that you don't ask God for
it" (James 4:2). Through this verse we can see
that prayer is not merely an available option, it is
a necessary action. Consider the wonderful truth
in these words: *God wills that we become
partners with him in seeing his promises
fulfilled.*

I once heard a well-meaning teacher say, "If
God has made a promise, you don't have to ask
him to keep it." The teacher wanted to make the
point that we don't have to beg God for things,
for he has already shown his intention of blessing
and providing for us. But, while this is true, it is
also true that most promises are not automati-
cally fulfilled apart from prayerful, humble
request. God can keep his promises, he wills to
keep his promises, but we need to come to him,
in prayer, with our requests. And it is equally true
that he wants us to become maturing sons and

daughters, who increasingly partner with him in the business of his kingdom through prayer and petition.

PRAYER: AS IT ADVANCES

God calls us to prayer, and Jesus commands us to pray, because it is in prayer that we move toward our highest place of partnership with him. In prayer, we can discover God's purpose that is to be fulfilled in each of us, in those we love, and in the community and world where we live. It is this purpose that draws us to follow Jesus' instructions in Matthew 6:9 to pray, "Thy will be done on earth."

But please stop for a moment and consider that phrase, "Thy will be done on earth," for here is an essential point that must not be missed, or our understanding of God's great purpose for us to join him in prayer will be seriously weakened.

With these words, Jesus teaches us that the target of our fellowship with God is that we would be led into partnership with him. God seeks people who will learn to walk with him and discover how much is possible when faith touches hands with the Almighty. When we see this, we can begin to believe that our praying for his will to be done on earth is actually possible! We will see that it is both our privilege and our responsibility to pray in this way, knowing that when we do so our prayers will be effective.

When you have entered into this prayer partnership with God, your daybreak meetings will move into a whole new dimension: the dimension of intercessory prayer. This type of prayer involves the high privilege of praying for others: for the great and small issues in the lives of people you know and of people you've never met. Intercession allows you and me to influence the world in which we live through the special power source of a prayer partnership with the Lord. Intercessory prayer is intimate, important prayer. It is a type of prayer that grows out of our having learned a daily fellowship with Christ.

And so you can see the entire span of prayer in the Lord's Prayer. You can see that requesting "daily bread" has to do with you and with me, while "thy will be done on earth" has to do with others—even entire nations. Thus Jesus' teaching takes us from the intimate, personal aspect of prayer to the equally intimate prayer of intercession: from fellowship to partnering in rulership.

And thus we have come full circle. If you will recall, when I began, I mentioned my alarm going off at 6:00 A.M., at which time I was getting up to pray. As I related, that was the day the Lord stopped me from the praying I was about to do (mainly intercession), and called me back to a renewal of a private, personal devotion habit.

Of course, Jesus didn't tell me to stop my intercessory praying, but he did want me to nourish the roots of my personal relationship and recultivate the qualities of warmth and intimacy with him. He was reminding me that no matter how much I may grow in learning the power of prayer in his name, I had to give my personal prayer-relationship with him top priority. I had to return to a daily walk that would keep me sensible, practical, and pure.

Such a daily walk would keep me from confusion, deception, and error. And such a walk would keep me growing in wisdom, love, and his character.

It will do that for you, too.

KEEPING PERSONALLY RELATED

Long ago Jesus made an observation about people who learn to use his power but who fail to walk closely and personally with him. He said, "At the Judgment many will tell me, 'Lord, Lord, we told others about you and used your name to cast out demons and to do many other great miracles.' But I will reply, 'You have never been mine. Go away, for your deeds are evil' " (Matthew 7:22, 23).

These words are a startling warning. They show clearly that Jesus isn't looking for people who serve powerfully at the expense of their personal relationship with him. Still, his words aren't intended to prevent us from expecting a power-filled life, nor to discourage us from power-filled prayer. For Jesus also said, "I have given you authority over all the power of the Enemy. Nothing shall injure you!" (Luke 10:19), and "[The Father] will give you what you ask for because you use my name" (John 16:23). So there *is* a pathway of power available to every believer who wants his life to grow to its fullest dimension in Christ.

But that pathway begins with spending personal, intimate time with him. For the deepest workings in our lives that will shape us into his image will take place when we are alone, keeping closely and personally related, in his presence.

That's where I urge you to go every day. And that's why I've sought to provide you with a practical, workable outline for going there. I hope it helps you to walk ever closer with Jesus, at daybreak and all day long.

CHAPTER SEVEN
SOME SHAFTS OF SUNLIGHT FOR YOUR DAYBREAK

The ideas on the following few pages are designed to assist your worship, praise, and understanding as you move toward a pattern of regular morning times with Jesus. All of these things are optional but one, and that one is reading God's Word. That is an absolutely essential activity, as I will explain soon. The other suggestions, I hope, will be helpful as your growing walk with the Lord Jesus expands. In any case, I pray that these pages will be bright shafts of sunlight, shedding additional radiance on your way.

DAYBREAK AND THE READING OF GOD'S WORD
This small book is focused on helping you establish a personal relationship with Jesus and

a presentation of your whole being to him each day. It is not intended to do anything more than that.

But I am deeply concerned that no one make the mistake that, since there is no specific pathway for reading the Word of God outlined, it is considered unimportant. Your use of God's Word on a daily basis is vital. It is foundational in developing your relationship with the Lord. Neglect of the Word will result in spiritual starvation for lack of food, just as neglect of prayer will result in spiritual suffocation for lack of air.

The regular use of the Bible is an activity on which all daily devotion must be based. And we must realize that reading and studying the Bible are two different matters. The former is like eating a meal; the latter is like analyzing your diet. The first nourishes, the second teaches you the principles of nutrition. Both can be developed in a fulfilling, profitable, and simple way (none of the basics of true spirituality are complex!).

Consider the exhortation of the Scriptures: "Read and explain the Scriptures . . . preach God's Word" (1 Timothy 4:13), and "This Book of the Law shall not depart from your mouth, but you shall meditate in it day and night, that you may observe to do according to all that is written in it. For then you will make your way prosperous, and then you will have good success" (Joshua 1:8, NKJV).

Read something from the Word of God every day. A basic and practical pattern is to give yourself ten to fifteen minutes for daily Bible reading, either split between the morning and the evening or all at once. With that time allotment, you will usually read the Bible through every year. And it often is best to read the Bible by reading whole books, as opposed to jumping around and sampling small portions of the Word without any coherent objective in mind.

It is usually helpful and often meaningful to make a practice of jotting brief notes to yourself as you read your Bible. Consider marking or highlighting verses or phrases that hold special meaning for you, and inserting footnotes that record thoughts the Holy Spirit makes alive to you as you read. These are timeless, worthwhile practices that have always been observed by God's people . . . so be encouraged to do the same.

These simple guidelines will help get you started. Just remember that spending time reading the Bible must be a top priority in your daily life with Jesus.

THE USE OF JOURNALS
One of the beautiful aspects of developing a close, daily walk with Jesus is that he talks with you. It is common that, as you wait before the Lord, he will teach you, bringing thoughts to your mind, helping you think more clearly about certain matters, opening your understanding to something you've been praying about or that you

read in his Word, and generally assisting you with practical insights.

For example, when you present your day to the Lord and outline the day's planned activities, you often will receive his counsel on specific matters. His helpful instruction often comes in a simple insight, an enlightened perspective, or a reminder from the Holy Spirit of something you already knew that will help you see the issue more fully. It's always a good idea to write these things down in a journal.

Writing these thoughts and insights will help you recognize and receive God's practical counsel. It isn't that these notes will contain some special inspiration, but it is useful to have them for reference as you go through the day. You can come back to the journal at the end of a week, a month, or even a year, and see quite clearly the ways God has responded to you and led you. Imagine how exciting and encouraging that would be!

You might also want to keep a personal journal. This can be a simple record of your feelings and thoughts as you go through your day. It doesn't need to be profound or poetic (though it certainly can be if you so desire), just honest.

Throughout the centuries, believers who have taken their walk with Christ seriously have made it a practice, when the Lord dealt with something in their lives, to write it down. Some have kept a daily journal, similar to a diary, but instead of writing down their daily activities they wrote down the insights they received each day in prayer and through the Word of God.

Others kept journals of specific occasions, when the Lord dealt with them in a special way or when they were simply pouring out their hearts to him in times of crisis, joy, hunger, need, or heartache. The Book of Psalms is a journal of sorts, for the Holy Spirit inspired people—David, mostly—to write out their heart-cries to God. Of course, these Scriptures were more than just a journal, for they were breathed into existence by the eternal Spirit of God expressly for our abiding revelation and edification. So when God speaks to your heart, or when your heart is crying out to him, it is practical and fulfilling to record those feelings through writing them down.

Sometimes your journal entries will throb with joy; other times they may be filled with pain. You may also express a commitment you are making in response to God's work in your heart, dreams you have discovered because of the faith he has stirred in your soul, or insights you want to re-member because the Holy Spirit made something of the Scriptures especially vivid and real to you.

Either way, whether you are just taking notes on a simple notepad while at prayer or making occasional entries in a more permanent book, let me invite you to walk the daybreak pathway as millions before you have done, responding and writing down the things the Lord Jesus puts in your heart.

THINKING ON THE NAME AND PERSON OF THE LORD

It was suggested earlier, on page 39, that you begin your praise and worship each day by thoughtfully considering God's attributes, ways he has revealed himself to you, and ways in which you need his power to work in your life. To help you do this, I am providing two lists that resulted from the meditations of two men, Dick Eastman and myself. I hope these lists will aid you in learning the full scope and privilege of using the resources given to us in the name of the Lord.

List One. Praise the Lord for the expressions of his Person so beautifully shown in these names or titles given to him in his Word. (These references were taken from the New King James Version of the Bible.)

DAY	NAME/TITLE	TRAIT/PROVISION
1.	A Scepter (Num. 24:16, 17)	Authority
2.	The Captain of the Hosts of the Lord (Josh. 5:14)	Victory
3.	The Rock of My Salvation (2 Sam. 22:47)	Defense
4.	The Lifter Up of My Head (Ps. 3:3)	Confidence
5.	The Headstone of the Corner (Ps. 118:22)	Support
6.	The Lily of the Valley (Song of Sol. 2:1)	Freshness

DAY	NAME/TITLE	TRAIT/PROVISION
7.	The Rose of Sharon (Song of Sol. 2:1)	Freshness
8.	A Great Light (Isa. 9:2)	Guidance
9.	A Nail Fastened in a Sure Place (Isa. 22:22, 23)	Security
10.	A Sure Foundation (Isa. 28:16)	Strength
11.	A Wall of Fire (Zech. 2:5)	Protection
12.	A Refiner and Purifier (Mal. 3:3)	Growth
13.	The Bridegroom (Matt. 25:10)	Affection
14.	The Bread of Life (John 6:35)	Nourishment
15.	The Way, Truth, and Life (John 14:6)	Purpose
16.	The Deliverer (Rom. 11:26)	Liberation
17.	The Power of God (1 Cor. 1:24)	Stamina
18.	The Wisdom of God (1 Cor. 1:24)	Enlightenment
19.	The Lord of Glory (1 Cor. 2:7, 8)	Majesty
20.	A Quickening Spirit (1 Cor. 15:45)	Energy
21.	The Head of the Body (Col. 1:18)	Supervision
22.	The Lord of Peace (2 Thess. 3:16)	Comfort
23.	The Brightness of His Glory (Heb. 1:3)	Ecstasy

DAY	NAME/TITLE	TRAIT/PROVISION
24.	The Express Image of His Person (Heb. 1:3)	Reality
25.	The Propitiation (1 John 2:2)	Forgiveness
26.	The Alpha and the Omega (Rev. 1:8)	Totality
27.	The Hidden Manna (Rev. 2:17)	Provision
28.	The Amen (Rev. 3:14)	Finality
29.	The Lion of the Tribe of Judah (Rev. 5:5)	Boldness
30.	The Word of God (Rev. 19:3)	Creativity
31.	The Bright and Morning Star (Rev. 22:16)	Awakening

List Two. The second list is included to illustrate something that may occur in your own life. Expect the Holy Spirit to give you surprise promptings that will expand the wonder and goodness of the Lord Jesus in your heart and mind. Jesus said of the Holy Spirit, "He shall praise me and bring me great honor by showing you my glory" (John 16:14). That is what happened with me.

I was at my devotional prayertime in New Orleans one Wednesday morning, and as I began to praise the Lord my heart was filled with a simple, overflowing idea from the Holy Spirit. As I began to worship, the thought came into my mind that I should praise God for his attributes, using words that began with every letter of the

alphabet. They came so readily that I knew God's
Spirit was assisting my praise.

I hope you will be edified and stimulated in
your own worship when you read through the list.

Lord God, I lift my heart to you because the
richness of your person commands my
highest devotion. I praise you because you
are:

Almighty—There is no power that exceeds
yours.

Beautiful—Your loveliness is shown in your
heart-gift of Jesus and your handiwork in
creation.

Creator—You are never limited by what is;
you can always do more than seems possible.

Dependable—You are there for every
situation I face.

Everlasting—You encompass my being
with your breath of life and love.

Fulfiller—Your Spirit overflows me with
hope and help for living.

Glorious—Because of you, a radiance
floods the ordinary.

Holy—The awesome completeness of your
being brings a new dimension to mine.

Immutable—Your unchanging nature comforts me in an everchanging world scene.

Jehovah—Your chosen name expresses your all-sufficiency, given to me.

Kind—As a loving father takes time for his children, so you take time for me.

Loving—This is true beyond human description or understanding.

Mindful—Your Word says you are always thinking about me . . . I'm overwhelmed.

New—In your gift of mercies every morning and in your constant working in my life.

Omnipotent—Nothing that tests my faith can limit your might and the strength you give me.

Precious—Your Word is like gold; your presence a treasure beyond value.

Quick—You never delay unnecessarily; you always answer me at the best time.

Righteous—Your justice and fairness deal life to each of us with lovingkindness.

Sensitive—Your heart is touched with my feelings . . . you care.

Terrifying—Not to me, Lord, but to the Enemy. He flees before you.

Undergirding—Your strong arm supports
me always, in all ways.

Victor—The triumph you have won over all
life and death is given to me, too!

Wonderful—In your character and in your
full-of-wonder doings.

X-cellent—Your ways and your being
transcend my finest imaginings.

Yesterday, Today, and Forever—You assure
me that every issue of my past, present, and
future is under your rule.

Zestful—Life has no dull moments when I
live it with you!

Other Resources

AUDIO CASSETTE TAPES
Related teachings by Jack Hayford are available
through the SoundWord Tape Ministry. The following is
a suggested list that correlates closely with the theme
of *Daybreak*.

TITLE	TAPE NUMBER
"The Renewal of Devotional Habit, Part 1"	2178
"The Renewal of Devotional Habit, Part 2"	2180
"The Renewal of Devotional Habit, Part 3"	2183
"The Problem of Spending Time in Prayer"	1224

Please refer to the tape number when ordering. These
audio cassette tapes, as well as a complete catalog of
tapes by Jack Hayford, can be obtained by writing to:
SoundWord Tape Ministry, 14300 Sherman Way, Van
Nuys, CA 91405-2499.

VIDEOTAPES
Videotapes for use in homes, Bible studies, small
group meetings, and churches may be special or-
dered. For information and a catalog of current listings,
please write to: Living Way Ministries, 14300 Sherman
Way, Van Nuys, CA 91405-2499.

Other Books by Jack Hayford

Along with *Daybreak* there are several other booklets in this series by Jack Hayford available from Tyndale House Publishers.

Newborn
Expressly prepared for the new believer as a clear statement of exactly what Christ's salvation and one's new birth involve. A practical guide for learning to walk and live in the family of God. This book also includes a simple but profound section dealing with the meaning and dynamic of water baptism. While written to the new believer, it is designed so that even the most advanced will discover fuller dimensions of truth about their resources in Christ since their water baptism.

Prayerpath
A new call has gone out around the world—a call to believers to unite in concerts of prayer, joining in faith for spiritual breakthrough on a global dimension. In *Prayerpath,* Jack Hayford takes readers step by step along the pathway of prayer, showing what Jesus taught about how to pray and how to live and grow in vital faith.

Spirit-Filled
Practical instruction on the person and power of the Spirit, teaching how, when, and where to put the spiritual gifts and graces to use in your life. Encourages the reader to open to the fullness of the Spirit of Christ and shows how to maintain wisdom and balance in daily Spirit-filled living.

The following book by Jack Hayford is also available from Tyndale House Publishers:

The Visitor
A study of the suffering of Christ that gives the reader an uncluttered insight into the reasons for and results

of Christ's visit to mankind. A perceptive, on-target treatment that enables readers to meet the Visitor face to face, recognizing his endless love and accepting his purpose and plan in their lives.

DATE DUE